Laddie Stardust

Laddie Stardust, Copyright, Ash Faith (Luis Rafael Baglietto Arce), 2018, All rights reserved.
Published in the U.S.A.

ISBN: 978-1719129602

Catopolis LLC
2390 Palisade Ave
4K
Bronx NY, 10463

Design and composition by Dallas Athent, dallasathent.com

Laddie Stardust

Ash Faith
(Luis Rafael Baglietto Arce)

To Star,
My big sis & muse.
This one's for you.
Here is to the bigger picture
& for holding my hand through the masses that compose its detail.

Acknowledgements

This compilation of poems written by Ash Faith, is an acknowledgement of his life. A life that as many of you know, has been filled with joy but also with many difficult obstacles, maybe too many obstacles for a young soul eager to live life, and filled with dreams and aspirations.
Ash Faith, is Luis Rafael's chosen name to go through life, and to be known as the author he aspires to become, and the name that inspired him and that embrace his faith in the power of love and miracles.
Ash could not write this acknowledgment, but he gave it the "Rock On" sign, so I am borrowing Ash's voice to write these lines of recognition to the people he would have liked to be acknowledged in a very special way, keeping in mind that all of you who came across his path were special to him.

"First, I would like to acknowledge my dearest friend Cat Bunny for making this book possible. Without her, this dream of mine would have not happened. I want to acknowledge my IDP (Interdependence Project) Community for not only being part of my journey, but having become part of my path. Your guidance, love and support during these last years has been an immeasurable source of strength, faith, and inspiration.
My partner and companion Lee, for your unconditional love and support. For holding my hand, for standing by me and with me along the way. I only wish I could have met you earlier but I know deep inside that I have met you at the right time, the time when I needed you the most. Thank you for being my soul mate during this life time...
I want to acknowledge my mama Lydia for her sweet love. From all her grandchildren, I was the one who knew her the most. I am the one whom she loves the most. Too many memories to named them. I know you will remember them for both.
My brother Stefano for being a witness of our childhood and a source of validation and love. To Ramiro, for caring, and for being there unconditionally. To my father and his family for taking the time to come visit when I could no longer visit them. Thank you for Paolo and Piero.

My cousins, Dea, Eli, David, Dylan and Machaella. Because I loved you all so much and making those trips to California to be with you and my tias and tios was a great source of happiness.

I want to acknowledge the one person who has been with me from the very beginning in this journey that has been my life: My mother-- "Madre" as I like to call her. Those of you who know me also know her. Beyond our meetings and departures, our ups and downs and our finding and loosing each other, my Madre has been there for me as a mother, as an advocate, as my voice at times, as the fountain of strength and courage I needed to drink from... I will always be in you, and you in me, in the lives to come. I love you my Madre....

I want to acknowledge you all who are reading this book, who have crossed your paths with mine. All of you who were part of the experiences that inspired these poems, and the pages of my journals... I just want you all to know that. I AM SO GRATEFUL THAT I HAVE CROSSED PATHS WITH YOU, THAT I LOVE YOU, AND THAT YOU ARE AWSOME"

-Written by Tia Nancy Arce-Wallach on behalf of Ash Faith (Luis Rafael Baglietto Arce).

Laddie Stardust: Rebellion.

AD: Angel Dialogue

**Angels? Where are you hiding your little halos?
You know… those little things surrounding edges of
happening, promising circles of happiness.**

Sometimes, I like to think that folks like you laugh at our urges, while somehow caring enough to let some of us live, learn, & love— from them.

Sometimes, I've heard people say that 'we can learn to turn by reforming our actions and intentions based on experience'. Yet sometimes I feel we'd rather not learn—but rather choose to breathe & simply rest whatever into oblivion.

3

Angels & Urges….

    I guess it only matters what mood you're in to even think about them.

**I've always been the type to avoid obstacles, when it's nothing more than rigorous & rigid.
Thinking to myself: Can we honor some self-sacrifice?
I guess it's all about keeping the channels of Faith (my favorite superhero!)
& Interactions,
open.**

**I think to breathe // & breathe to think
Hiding behind the damaged silence
through clutters of
destruction // distraction // experience
determined to survive it.**

'Why are you absent now, Sweet Angels?
Are you busy Hiding // Seeking/ /Interacting
in recipes creating
A desire for delirium // A delirium for desire,
helping me Taste a sense of divinity--
     Restless, Rapid, & Innocent....'

Sometimes I feel them responding:

We're not absent & you're not hopeless. We can give you what you witness for experience but your methods must come from within.

 Don't depend on Salvation as the higher force--

   Become what you wish
   & we will serve you the final dish.

 That's awesome. I love ripping through riddles & I'm hungry.

Cocteau Divine

Once upon a time,
I jump in my car to turn on the soul sparks of sight & sound.
My Cute Little Hyundai's got an aptitude for connecting a rush
beyond being bound by solitude. It diminishes a sense of desperate
isolation by diving into impulse & ignoring consequence, because
everything counts as an experience.

The truth is, it never mattered how old I was—5, 15, 20—I always
seemed Present yet "Missing"—Always wanting to live a real life
distraction while discovering this thing people call "boundaries," to
define what's real or unreal.

I always felt that when dreams become a hot-ride,
their morning breeze can transform into warmth on overcast
mornings.
I conquer a sense of sunshine as fresh scent,
ambitious & anxious with existence,
in a haze, knowing night as day while it's too dark to say it is.
I blast Industrial, Metal, & Shoegaze;
embodying lyrics that fluctuate between confusion, adrenaline, &
empathy—
brewing connections to "conscientious" questioning.

Is this what all that, *"you're such a one of a kind individual"* essence fuss is
about?
Can I crave something a little more?

I'm bored
As a Mysterious Skin enveloped by galaxies of rapture & reciprocity,
answering curiosities for a psyche craving self-discovery
in any city—
Bred beyond surrendering to it
by being here, there, everywhere,
& anywhere…but here.

(Ride—Drive Blind)

Pikachu Zero Signal

I start preparing for photo shoots to be masked & nude,
while daydreaming & asking,

"Where am I?"

My psyche clings to the ideal courage,
confident & doubtfully responding:
*"**showing your bare bones which other boys don't care to touch.**"*

Ugh, that's the latest Rye said anyway. I think it's still funny that we've been fleshing out on & off for the past 4 years, with him whining, me responding, & both of us wishing numbness over this thing called...?

Then he gets all face divine with sides of sarcasm & cruelty, dropping fear bombs to my psyche like a parasite.

I show him the opposite & let my unconscious stir an understanding in worth & rebellion.
Lately it's just been a matter of absorption.
No failures // No conquests.
Just a main focus:
exercising "potential,"
by consuming contemplation,
wishing to externalize the internalized.

All these little thoughts for a little framed dude, racing to figure out the value & truth behind everyone's face
                    faith
                    game
                    gain.

              equal to you.

I get nude, stare at the walls & bare my all for these things called:

Flashing Photography & Artistry.

All this in honor of my little bud neighbor, whom snagged my first pictures randomly & genuinely by asking me to conquer a confidence he saw but I didn't.
Then chance brewed this thing that went beyond flirting & got our mouths to turn randomly down during a photo session.

We went our ways after good gracious fun & feeling,
but then again that's how it always is flesh.

My soul feels like an electric baby blue blanket swimming in sensory discovery, thinking **what's the point of adding so much to things that are simply meant to be?**

I pose for a stance while wondering,

Where am I & What am I becoming?

I toss any traces of shame serving any empty substance, feeling heavy on my light body—
Letting the flashing capture of art class assignment happen.

I spent about a decade decoding & resisting
from all types of styles,
once seen as restricting.

Habits are a haunting for me & I'm perked to just breathe &, know that I've partied so much in countless streets, while being safest in sound & never bound.

Most of my life, I feel safe when experiencing my friends or strangers playing lifeguards.
They take me under their wing before a sense of "Awareness" strikes their faces from smiling in disconcerting discoveries.
Even if its quick or takes some time, they always seem to notice I need help
in growing up, while taking it easy, as we wonder what's worthy….

Sometimes they care enough (especially Star) to give cautionary sound advice…& other times they—(especially Big Brother)—just seem to wonder: **WHY!?!?!?,** when I do something that doesn't make sense to them,

I guess I'm just so electrified by the basic goodness in everything, I choose exploring some eye rolling stunts because of it.

Self care…
I'd rather dodge it by pretending I don't need it & just be protected.
I love my family and friends because I learn from their experiences, as well as mine with them.
'A love my way type' of caring,
cured by the warmth of psychedelic furs in bedroom hour volumes.

    The process of unwinding is a twirl of twisted splendor.

I go to shows to understand Electricity erupting from unspoken emotion, driving "silent shouts" by letting loose in charged grounds soaking up the sounds in terrains of dizzy times & dog day sunshine like Blood, Milk, & Sky // "Kaleidescope & Candle eye"// candy like cravings.

I always thought limits were boring, even though I felt dumb lucky with some of the things I've gotten away with.

All I know about "growing up" is that the art of Learning can DEF lead to a divine touch when you rip through the nonsense of static confusion.

I have a friend named Mel Belle that says rain is supposed to mean new things.
Meanwhile, I'll quietly think about how new things can block you out from any 'old small things', waiting to be patiently completed.

Even when I want to experience something a little more conquering than feeling haunted or hungry, I see the craving as nothing short of serendipitous—leading to adventure or ambition… outweighing

through the sensitivity of

seeping through the glassy shards of cracked conflict in scattered ground.

It's funny how I can see things, sometimes….

411

Catered by loving parents paving their own paths,
I was once a boy created by chance,
who felt like any moment, could be his last;
always daydreaming of inevitable attack & invincible defense
while crossing paths with Love & Vision.

I have a little brother named Stef.
We're split by a decade & he's already overcome his first one.
He's my little troop, following my or our parents' examples, while
paving his own through flexible standing.

I think of my Big Sis Star in the city streets,
Cars speeding past her,
locked in the stare of her lost soul.
We always sink into gradual grounds,
soaked with the experience of flowing friendships,
producing a breezed charm—
wandering through the masses in search of the bigger picture,
striving for realizations in the future features of blissful fortunes
blessed in rest,
turned to dusk,
founded by the sun...
eating Cuban sandwiches outside the Batcave since they won't let me in.

Nico fuels us in Gemini essence
leading us through blunt honesty composed by soul, love, & a sheer
sense of family in order to flourish our souls fluorescently.

Xio shows us to enjoy the unknown through And One.
She's Star's dazzling jazz twin who cures herself with hopeful
resilience & hopeless romance. I don't know her like the others
except that we both bear
a caramel curiosity swirling through communities while not being
bound by them.

I'm the baby boy with lots to learn & more energy to burn.
Comfort is the hidden chance we seek, sinking us into the fluid

confidence underneath our dreams,

unearthed by experience.

I think of all the times we spend together;
coming across dreamy terrains of laughter, love and unison; lacing our curiosity in boundless fusion.

Choosing landscapes to embark in:
Bedroom >> Bus travel Cities >> Clubs >> Concerts >> Adventures
Together or Separate,
constantly confiding
redefining
wishes & re-COGnition,
in a haze of happenings.

We dine & drink in spots that supply intrigue through dim lit rooms & darling faces
lighting up company.
Some with names or a sense of grace that occupies whatever phase we're in:
always counting our connections as genuine.
They like us the same ways we are drawn to them,
since it's all about connecting with essence in the end.
Yet our minds never fail to remind us how to Remain confused
in some magnetized lure by Reversing, reacting & re-enacting past scenarios of repeated wonders, **believing in the unrest.**
Our character is split by beats of zip fear,
quenched thirst,
& the cracked bones of comfort posture.

::::Cranes—Paris & Rome::::

Lost & Fun

"Crystal Method—Alive Alone"

Initially I could be imagined as the dude with impaired reflexes,
Not beyond repair but rather recognized by pairs of jubilant eyes & endless jive,
fused by what's unique, wise, & nothing short of a joyride.

"He has so much potential… so consciences… but never going beyond the challenge," all my teachers use to mention about me during parent teacher conferences.

I walk the streets to breathe in a thrill seeking consciousness in love with sequences of synchronicity, being an oddity with the ability to defy the odds while always on the trail for an array of fun.

       Ambition, Innocence, Standard, Expectation, Exploration Rebellion, Restlessness:

                 Call it what you want.

       I'll be Dreaming of the unborn chance & try to make a reality out of it

Kingdom

Sitting below the cube on Cooper Square, staring at the
St. Marks dip strip.
Surrounded by strangers
(yet already ran into someone I knew)
I notice lovers flocking in unison,
reminded of how I tend to give my body away to disposable memory
rather than quality destiny:

Surrendering to others as a mere episode of experience by repeating compulsions;
flushing flustered innocence in flashes of discovery.

::(tie into first date at St. Marks with Lee later in the story)::

My imagination imitates burnt out fascination of fueled assumptions,
dwelled by disappointment. I crave to escape inside the dead ideals,
too empty to feel.

Sometimes I wish I bared the simplicity of other boys, but then I
reflect on how I live my life:

Living enough to know the unexpected is essential:
All those times in the backseat of a moving bus, guided by all types o' thought--
blasting musical triggers to any mental spots that wonder about limits & wish for
evolution- Mechanized like a body hammer bass pedal racing into resolution.

Vid Ivo Kid.

Polar opposite mixtures raised me,
by brewing a sense of image & flavor to promote a sense of possibility within any community.

My dad would always share with me that it's something adults are supposed to do, while surprising me at a nearby video store by allowing me to see things out of my reach.

I think of those childhood days,
always kept safe from being in harm's way
in front of form radiating visual rays

My true blues are rooted in feeling like a fool craving a clue, & answered curiosities.
I like gazebos because they make me feel safe within a gaze,
while reminding me that Hopes & Dreams are never too late---even if recognizing that running into them is scarier on the inside than the outside may show.

Kind of like those times you hear stories of chance & spark a wish or 2 for your own to come true; letting the a sheer wish that forms a happening to have you wonder
how to break a routine // bend out the boredom // & become a worthy being, shaped by

substance, function, & efficiency

My mind gets curious when
I imagine coordinated motion arising from stillness

Seeping through the glassy shards of cracked ground

& walking this rectangular ground while floating above any grinding thoughts by putting my heads in the clouds.
From the images of my mind's eye
white, black, & lavender blues bring red roses too!
& then comes those white steps
centered in my path,
waiting to be walked on.

Climbing up the center
the flowers keep on blooming.
Every step taken
pulsing a new existence.

Then you come along
out of nowhere
from anywhere
that is a somewhere.

It's funny how I can see things sometimes.

"*Good//Clean//Fun*"

TINKER BELL

She warned me not to go to the show with her because I wouldn't enjoy myself.

She was right.

Some brats preach and rant about no drugs or meat while promoting a positive message in overkill tension.
The show ends >> I voice my craving for a steak >> & peace.

"You never listen to me!," she yammers in obvious disappointment.
"I was bored & curious!" I retaliate, knowing she got a free ride out of it anyway.

Tinker Bell is my little firecracker of brown skin & ambition—knowing she deserves the best because she was raised to never settle for less.

Still bored, I drive in a daze of disappointment.
Later calling my folks high on white,
watching the sun rise in

A blaze of emotion all stirred up.

Apathy is my numb safety that hides value in the present tense. My wheels sheer against the pastures of grass-trimmed roads. Highlighting colors in rooftops & design. I'm in the middle ground of scrapped illusion & phased conclusion:

Wanting something more than the double bass pedal of road time adrenaline & the surrounding rounds of friends embracing disappointment for destiny.

Pikachu

Nico rescued me with a random sleepover at her place.

We fall asleep to The Cure & wake up to the song "Burn";
I used to spend my childhood daze listening to it while dreaming of being old enough to watch _"The Crow"._

I can't help but feel it's going to be a decent day.
Sometimes memories feel like a treasure yearning to be grasped, thriving off nostalgia and wishful thinking—creating a gratification that's filled with grasping to a craving that can't compare with the present moment.

Maybe that's why I write-to record, interpret & never forget it.

> **There are 24 hours during the day.**

Half of it becomes wasted by distraction
Some becomes wasted by responsibility
communicating honestly.

I have this constant desire for a miracle to happen & sometimes wonder if I've got some higher force looking over me—laughing or shaking their head because I'm only 20 & young having experienced so much
(& so little)
compared to others.

I'm so lucky to have the people I love,
a roof over my head,
& a life to embrace with electric grace.

Zero-Signal

I have dreams, ambition & intuition, yet can't seem to rock a sense of structure
because spontaneous flames, that are nothing but fueled joyrides,
crash my taste buds by numbing them.

Not caring for those who care about you is RIDICULOUS.
I lay with the longest lover & feel a numb routine
He opens his doors to me with kisses as I sleep,
whispering
"you can stay as long as you desire."

I smile with disguise
& think of a more current lover
who swept through me
& exited.

In this daze,
physicality overpowers connecting
& all I know about connecting with quality
is that looking straight into a person's eye
gives an encounter more impact.

Tokyo Vogue

I'm in a Boutique that's small in size with imperial design.
I work for a woman with a youthful mindset.
A creator in her own age with the experiences of a sage.
It's nice coming out to the recent breeze of
Spring Air to work in Ms. Holley's shop.

Yet in the silent wisps of whiplash doubt—I feel like I could or should be doing so much more.

My fresh friend, Tokyo Vogue, tells me not to be ashamed:
"Life can totally be a lot worse & you're just left craving a high valued essence when anxiety and expectations crash your psyche.
In -tensions
of **cut // throat // competition"**

Ms. Holley reveals:
" it's not dull to work at a mall the way some people do, because it's all they can."

Nico reminds:
"you gotta beat retail hell, ditch your shell & come out on top"

Who am I? What am I? What will I be? What can I be?

The perks of sunny day contemplating in this fresh decade called Twenty

---

A cute woman with curly short hair & a flower dress, named Honey,
came to show her love & connect with Miss Holley.

She was the 2nd person today to look at me & ask if we're related, revealing:

" You have such a pleasant presence in the boutique."

I felt like telling her Perks & Productivity entice my insides since
demons used to take my mind as a child, rocking me back and forth
in apathetic delight.

But instead I smile & thank her for the boosting compliment.

My habits know I crave to escape when time feels wasted within my daze,
which is why, I'm always sure to go out when the sun is down.

I'm given free time to create or destroy
but only swallow the phases where I find stimulation as a full degree,
experiencing the building blocks of memory.

Then there's a collision of shame and gratitude—
Always wanting what we can't have yet mourning the loss of what we did have,
loving recognition
in its embrace.

A little boy with sun colored hair & sky tinted eyes runs around the boutique
thriving off the eye candy juices in his mind.
He looks at me and waves & point at my cuff
in jibberish jubilance.
When I ask what he's saying,
his mom replies:

"Your guess is as good as mine."

He sure did have life.

Afterwards, two fashionable sisters from Westchester named Abby
and Brenda, conversed with me about community & our history with
Miss Holley.

Abby is a teacher & told me to never lose my ambition.
I affirm that it's driving force which keeps me going.
& she confirms

"Ms. Holley is such a foundational teacher"

Signs >>> encounters >>> enlightenment.

A set of eccentricity, came into the store with a thick-wheeled bicycle and basket attached to the handle. She made Ms. Holley a beautiful scarf with radiant colors intertwining its black base. She said the frays represent the future paths we follow in life—

"thick & thin within experience"

Youth Decay
Sunday.
It's the last night before school begins.
I get really stoned to Arcade Fire
& cruise a mall amped
to screen Grindhouse with a crowd of friends…later than me.
On my way to the theatre entrance, I envision myself as a loner, missing out on the crowd:

"welcome to the pack buddy" says a stranger with arm around a sympathetic looking dame.

How ironic.

Supergirl, Mandigo, & Danni-Gem arrive in no time,
with sides of alcohol to refresh my popcorn.

Planet Terror gets better
Death Proof makes adrenaline speed feel so sweet..

We all arrive to my car & pack a bowl to smoke since empty parking lots
always seem like easy game. We were so wound up over how good the movie was we parked behind am electrical fortress while Supergirl called her college bud demanding a screening attendance.

In the midst of high alert for security and cops, I notice a flurry of yellow sirens moving our luck. We jet our spot into another lot & everyone p[anics] over my driving rather than the chances of police following. We cruise through deciding to smoke & drive along the mall.

I suddenly have a change of heart & turn around towards a diner. Mandigo thinks its dumb while Sara thinks its smart.

Too bad I went the wrong way…

Everyone freaks out in the midst of red lights & doing time.

It's my turn to take a hit & I signal left while cruising between both lanes of an empty road. I stop at the red light and take my chances letting my neurons dance.
The light turns green & Mandigo screams
"WE'RE GONNA GET PULLED OVER!!!"

I have another change of heart & decide to take the next left.

"I know exactly where I'm going"
"What are you doing?!"
"I know where I'm going"

We're at an alternate parking lot entrance & comes across another light.
Danni Gem hands me the pipe
holding it tight for me to breathe.
A blue pickup truck comes our direction & the light turns green.

I STILL haven't taken my hit.

"We're going to get pulled over !!
We should've just smoked in Supergirls car!!!,"
Mandigo screams.

"Shut up dick weed. I know where I'm going."

Silence. Red light. I crouch
& take a hit
shortly kicked.
"see guys that wasn't so bad was it?"

"I don't know what you do but you keep doing it and don't get arrested. You don't have any problems with the law, do you?
You should've been arrested at least 25 times…" Supergirl recites.
"No Not really" I reply.
"You got some magical powers man. I want what you got & then market it."

"Yeah dude. I really don't know how you do it but you're the best at getting away with it." Mandigo peacefully interjects.

We pass another cop & stop by Supergirls Corolla.
I give everyone a solid exit 5
& Mandigo looks at me with a smile saying
"it's because you look so innocent."

I smiled wider watching my friends transfer before I drive.
Open window // music blaring
A cop following my lead.

The open window & chilled air
kills the scent of a single cop
hot on my trail.
I'm on 40 doing 45.
the limit turns 30 while I gradually slow for the red light

Cop car still on my trail…

Another car's in front of us
leaving us space in between.
The cop intersects,
tailgating in front of me

Brake light blinking
Over & over.

Turning right at hilly backroads
Finally off my trail.

Adrenaline is so sweet @ 30mph.

"Chai-thing"

After tasting my first cup of chai tea brewed by Belle—Tinkers baby sister—whose a venom glanced princess dwelling in moshpit relationships, & catching up to grownups by grownups before they can catch her—,

that I could never know how romance because I'm to busy mastering the mystery.

Cute.

I finish my chai & say goodbye.

Protégé distance

Time seems so reconstructed these days.
I hope it's all the growing times as of late.

I enter the subway & for the first time in 21 years of being raised and venturing in the city:
                I read a subway map & understand it perfectly!

I'm somewhat distraught by bland strangers with dry expressions as *"Real Eyes"* by Babes in Toyland screeches in my ears.

I decide to take the extra mile for the green platform & notice the handsome lean machine waiting for the train too.

We hear it from a distance
& decide to hop out of our current platforms
                Wrong train // we both remain

I distract myself by looking elsewhere,
glimpsing a glance while shouts are screamed to my ears—
      As I notice the lean machine
    dancing & choreographing his moves
          to whatever tunes

shift his groove,

He smiles in swift grace,
shameless & queer.
Vicious reminders of a past I fear,

He dances until the following stop & sprints in between divided doors.

I curse out loud
burning dirt in dick pit resentment.
// *you think you got it bad now…wait til you reach sucker-love climax* //
(I)ntuition whispers

I turn toward a platform exit and pass by a couple—
one hand over the others waist
a blending of head & shoulders.

I'm single & dazed
in flaky sight exits
& cupid resistance

I walk a tunneled maze to get to my R train,
stepping over scattered pages of Raptures
destined to consume our days.
All that silly hysteria postponed to never…
// Explosions & Destruction for some construction //
I'll never let control me.

I get to the platform and walk to a bench at the end.
A bum is asleep while his hands are buried in the waistline of his pants.

I sit behind him on the opposite side
& notice a card saying
"SUCCESS"
at the very end.

The R train comes
& by the time I reach my stop,
I'm the only one left on the train to an old home.

Bothering a Big Bro

"Uhhey,,, what's up man?"
" Hey dude… thanks for letting me stay so late"
"Yeah, no worries…"

What can I say about Big Bro? A couple of years in catholic school & being total opposites we seem to have this undying brohood quality. I admire his self- sufficiency the same way he seems to wonder about why I'm so prone to injury… & in love with Freddy Krueger & Buffy.

Sidewalk Sale

On an escapade with Supergirl
selling clothes and tarot card rants
for 5 bucks a pop.

I sold a shirt to trans punk rocker named Razor X
who was impressed by me & Supergirl's taste,
while talking music & fashion
in good graces
& the common thread of,
Once Upon A Time
I was bored and let some people call me Razors

Star came by & I read her cards, a few doors down, in a SWEET bar.
We rejoiced in fortunes luck
as Supergirl flew up to join our fun:

All 3 of us blending a conversation on survival from shitty people,
casual drug use,
& horror movies

"*A hug from a devil or a Bullet from an Angel*"

A bum approached me with a fairy tale:

"Once upon a time, I was in $500 debt & needed to raise 2 kids"

I got naive and imagined how horrible his situation might be.

The problem with beggars is that they're another body in a city of countless ones.
They could be lying
or they could be trothing.

    That makes them just like very other human

    except they live off the mercy of others >>>

    Weighing on the ignorance of full exposure
                  For better or worse.

    I give him 2 dollars and wished him a merry day.

    he says I have a good heart and god will bless my soul

              In complete sincerity.

    Video stores are such postuaries.

Ring around
I spend the night with Star.
Walking full circles around Midtown.
Picky with food & searching for Supergirl
we catch up endlessly & all I can do is appreciate her genuine warmth.

We head to Lennon's birthday party in Brooklyn—exploring the

fashions of sharp wit & heavy metal.
We make a 1:30am entrance where everyone graces her presence while she makes sure I'm not left out.

Lennon is observant while rolling up fresh blunts & a variety of drinks in streams of rock n' roll foresight. A world expanding glimpse of Stars shine—The only thing I can gather from her is that she sticks to her roots & loves hard.

We leave the party & hop on 3 trains to get back to the Bronx.

I sit across from her & she tells me I would be happier if I choose the right ways to settle in confidence. Knowing what she meant, I felt strangely read by an angelic love that sees me lost in doubtful cloud by wanting me to ditch the wrong things right.

I close my eyes for brief moments while dreaming of little things unknown

while our souls awaits to awake

—Laddie&star pic—

Astor Daze 06

I force myself to sleep,
recollecting memories that always make the dream.

I dreamt of a paradise within the masses I a crowded street.
Supergirl was by side & we rejoiced in the companies of strangers and friends,
wandering the city & passing through a club named Roxy.

Everyone's waiting for a grand time but I'm denied entrance because of a baby face & legal age.

I don't stick around for exemption & just turn around from its entrance.

Supergirl & I walk into a building, remodeled with shades of grey and different hallways.

It was our old school.

We smiled at the nostalgia and walked into a sunny day.
Tranquil & Timeless,
we walk towards a fountain with wide space and shining allure.

I looked up into the sky & notice the bridge above me.
It looked just like the Tappan Zee;
A beautiful sight visible from a distance behind the windows I call home.

The bridge then seemed to split in half,
& the water beneath it rose up and became a toy with the sky.

We moved back panicking & noticed the building we once called school,
from a distance.

The water began to soar to new heights & cars fell from the sky
in parallel velocities matching in reverse...

Reggie pushed me out of the way & the 3 of us dodged the cars and headed towards the building.

As each car missed us by inches, I could somehow sense a force looking after us,
making sure we made it out alive—always stepping on the right spots.

We finally reach the school & a rusted flag pole rises up from the ground and scrapes my arm. We try to get into the building but the doors are chained shut & the man cleaning the halls would not open it for us. The ground begins to shake & I punch through the window, breaking glass and ignoring the blood on my hands; creeping through confined space by making it to sanctuary.

The wounds didn't matter—we were safe.

ManicThrill00

Alert and Awake,
in a sense that even your soul feels it

as the soil happening.

You ignore consequence but figure there has to be another
up to your down // like there is another down to your up.

Sometimes the realization can shatter the energy of within your soul shimmering, an energy of distracting melody with smoky habits and drinking comforts—smoking creations of liquid hydration.

So I'll do all of the above and write because it's the most honest comfort and distraction to the emptiness of standing still during this thing I hear called

Enlightenment.

I feel the numbness of crashing & turned to the page against pen,
Reflecting on any moments that should be recorded.

Hours of loneliness in remedies of comfort,
I close my eyes in brief moments dreaming of little things so small.
that when my pulse rushes back to the waking world—It remains unknown.

I could write all day if I wanted.
I avoid writing because as much as I become unleashed in the experience of it,
    I fear the ideal of matching it up
      & comp(l)eting the feel.

Supergirl was my only catch during the gay pride today.
So I kill time with her & head to Barnes and Noble before my bus shows up.

The wooden steps leads us to wooden floors with creaking noise becoming balanced by our poise. I quietly wonder why shelves of books aren't being occupied, by people that should be occupying its space, by devouring knowledge instead of each other.

They say the most surrounded people are the loneliest.
It's true.
We're internally trapped
from the external glow
which seems to wrap us in a quality show.

We don't thrive off our own company the way self-respecting people should.

That's why I've been coming here since I was 15.

To fill the void & thrive

NEW PALTZ: 60 Main Street

Soft spoken Tobias, offers me a drink free of charge telling me that Destined tranquility is such a wondrous feeling.

I sit on the café couch
waiting away through the sweet aftertaste of steamed water smoking the atmosphere.
I feel like I have a lot to say but not enough energy to explain.
I can talk about the current tastes of liberty, my lusts for a love,
& my untouched shield of not settling for the next lame thing.

Tobias offers comfort, conversation, & an invite to his cinema political night for a flick called

"Corporation."

**A raw compilation of suffering, invasion, & corruption—
exploding warscape into wonder:**
what is the universal purpose of your fucking cause?

I could peacefully fall asleep
in the midst of stranger collisions,
running rampant in embrace.

2006

The Law wants to own everything & what scares me is that when they do
our mind is next.

Chelsea Hotel

July 3rd 2006

My eyes spring open to blossom relaxed.
Everything operating at a peaceful pace.

Mom takes me on a random shopping spree
& I finish a collage on government corruption—blurring exploitation
& liberation.

The sun begins to scorch
& I swim in solitude
in the midst of strangers under the sun.

Lifegaurd eye candy looks over my
wishful thinking in smooth thrive dives
looking all fine.

I read Charles Mansons autobiography,
pool side & bronzed,
under the sun.

In no time I hop on a bus
to save my heart & soul in dinners
with mom & grandma.

Crazy to think how dinner is an annual occasion these days.

We meet at Red Lobster,
voicing enthusiasm over upcoming trips to see Grandpa Raf.
Then I get a generational gang up on my shameless weed habit
by trying to convince him to ease his nerves with me.

I think it's cute
& fuse on the food
of being loved & blessed
With them by my side.

We drop mom off at the bus station & speak of his
mannerisms,
distinguished,
by brilliance.

Grandma talks about his arms
& mom talks about his stamping stomp whenever he didn't get his
way.

I meet with Supergirl & Sensual Steve for drinks & night joy
Which lead to meeting Dash & his new boy toy.
They take us to their room in Chelsea Hotel,
to pregame a party past sunrise.

Supergirl & I drag our eyes to exhaust,
 impulsively asking him if we can sleep in the bed while they dance
the night away.

Dash laughs
& lets me stay
// disappearing in dashing grace.

Supergirl & I touch the bed presence of our dreams,
& make it out in time for hotel checkouts & bus streams.

We walk under the sun of neon glows
to "fade away and radiate"
a Blondie fate
being fainty in daylights glow for our boundless souls

divided by bus terminals.

I get off my home stop & find a black feather
glistening on the ground.

After 4 hours of sleep, I stumble into my bathroom only to randomly find the cutest caterpillar. My irrational fear of bugs would've killed it at a quick glance, but instead I attempt to guard it with a glass & set it free to settle against a wall.

I shower with a peace of mind knowing it's stillness won't harm me & become fascinated by it's disappearance moments later,

I get to my car & notice a moth aching to get through the closed window of my passenger seat. I set it free into the breeze—knowing nothing is ever what it seems.

Life is a series of

while language is creations recipe for remarkable silence.

My phone rings & Mom replies in tears

"Grandpa's passed"

Rapid stillness pulses my veins.

"Ballad of a Lady Man"

A beautiful boy with earth tones prophet eyes, introduced himself to me.
We clicked instantly & like all the other faces, he claimed mine to be familiar.

We spoke socially, poetically,
& casually sexually.

I looked into his eyes & tried to gather what was in his mind.
In reactive radiation, he reveals:
"I can read fortunes & fallouts."

He read Booboo & Boo
with a ripe sense of accuracy

then he looks at me and says :

"Your barriers are beyond concrete
with lovers to your heart
bowing at your feet.

Some will think they're close
but aren't even close to connecting at its beat.
Your loved ones are disposed
with love & deceit.
You walk two paths
safe & seldom / / manic wisdom
As white gold colors of perception.,
always fearing deception.

You bear the mark of a warrior and sage,
fueling the lure of future endures

thriving off your wisdom
before you can even sense it scent."

An ode to positivity

We open our doors and windows to soak the breeze of contact with
absent shield.
We marvel at innocence
seeking to posses
it's charming arms
of gone doubt alarmed.

If we want to talk about sonic optimism,
let's talk about Lily Positive.

The spunk spirit of her timeless exterior
melts away your guarded interiors
with a genuine embrace
All too great

Deep Blue

I had my first good dream in a long long time
on the blue couch which showed me

a pattern of stripes // & colors
floating in the clouds
of dazzling heaven above—

Transcending up north.
There is motion in stillness.

I walk rectangular grounds
floating in the clouds
into a gaze colored haze
of divide & unite.

From these images of my minds eye
the flowers bloom
White, black, lavender
& red roses too!

I just know they're all poppin into livelihood..
& then comes those white steps
centered in my path
waiting for my grasp
climbing up the centers
of flowers bloomin' past.

Every step pulses a new existence.

Then you come along
out of nowhere
from anywhere

that is a somewhere.
& you give me that confident smile
rarely given by the strongest of men

whispering passing volumes to my ear.

Entangled eyes towards heads and heat.

The rest is a blurred elixir of taste
unique in quality & soul

I feel blessed again
& I think it's a constant reminder from those angels up above
sailing our bodies
to & from.

Volts

There is something awfully tricky about grasping onto something concrete
in the middle of unfolding layers of fate.
Unique thought is celebrated because it taps into the most common desires through the most uncommon methods

exercised into the eyes of a collective.

Star & I discover each other in rejoiced presence, remembering things only seen by us.
We hold this to ourselves, expressing it through various shape and form.

We hide from masses of false joy,
Thriving & laughing at the face of a challenge
when blind comfort takes control.

A few weeks later, I visit a monster in prison
& head to a Peruvian restaurant.
I was amazed at how the owner caters to my mother's elegance with striking emphasis.

She tries to teach me the ways of her charm & to be mindful of manners in very motion
with a strong priority.
I welcome it when I'm not raging to resist it.
I like to assume I don't need lessons… even though it's always an

honor to receive them.
We share the streaks of stubborn fuss, living out sides of our life with karma perks & high voltage anxiety, fueled by the genuine sincerities of guardian angels

Whispering intuitions
taking flight
In our mind.

Redline

Redline dives you far enough
to get all graspy with a workout
talking through thoughts

There is nothing more gripping than being lost.
I see a void & dare to look
We have a solution for every equation wrapped into

I care to dance in a furnace of whirlwinds,
set to gather thoughts
Of taste, sound, and pulse.

I saw 2 marvelous ladies perform a duet last night.
It was an unexpected sight of fire and water,
Intermingling melodies
Under the red lights
Of bright intensity

I let the wind guide me to the next crowd
& somehow I always knew a person standing in the steps ahead.

I felt a pull & followed through
with imagination stimulating thought.
Everyone's wasted
while claiming they love / .

I sit here relaxed
Re-wiring the constitutions of thought
& 1:30 wakeups.

Mom tells me to ease it down but I always feel that something remains unfinished.

I defy correction for fear of losing climax
I defy expectation for fear of losing correction
I embrace climax for fear of losing connection.
In the thrill of unborn experience.

Pulp

Solitude & study
seem to be the only things honest right now.

M & Jux help enjoy the peaks of synchronicity
while I hold onto tabs of acid in my white framed Dior box,
Waiting for the sun to roast our skins as one.

I'm reading some Kerouac,
Bombarded by silly prose while absorbing some of my own.

Laced drips // burning dirt

Phenomenon doesn't have to be inherently good or bad // Ice cream doesn't feel pleasure from its own side // Every experience comes about from what you do to someone else // karmic seeds rise up from what you perceive // the seed that ripens is similar to the one planted // mindfulness eradicates an afflicted state of mind // sex with wisdom starts with being conscious of what you planted in the past // use mindfulness to attain a useful state // The art of patience says people that irritate you are seeds in the process of being purified & eagerness diminishes the essence of your current life // Addictive behavior is a void being substituted & filled // Meditation brings the mind back to it's object // If you feel that your failing in falseness just remember the perks of practice come with true discipline

I surged in taboo
& crashed into little crumbles of shame.

He made sure I was fine
& I was lost as to why I would let his thick body over mine
Thick hands
& scented scant
Composing an unmentioned past.

Beauty

To be insatiable is to be desired but never conquered even by the best.

Beauty seems to interact under the colliding dynamics of chance.

Star.
Big sis grew out her hair
& glows even brighter with age.

Everyone evolves into something even if it may be nothing.
I'm infused with energies being stored & not used
while cluttering in the habits of false attachment.

Carrying outward // riding inward.

I'm not used to showing affection
nor am I used to being a property of someone else's.

Thrill numbs the nice side
while guilt settles on the other.
In my self-righteous blaze,
I say with heartfelt honesty
Intensities,
need only apply.

New Order
A short day at work brings all kinds of rewards.
Nico, Shilpa, & I
wander in Peep
to eat & wonder
why others are bothered

when we're surrounded.

Serious sensitivity always takes hold in unintended misperception,
making tenderness an inevitable treasure
craving erasure.

Nico, Jux, & I
dipped into the sips & smiles
of shroom-style tea
on a sunny Wednesday
at the Boiler Room
:::Wiper—Amusement Parks on Fire:::

I bid farewell to the batch,
packing them in cupcakes for
flavor & vision
to hatch
in the crumbs of afternoon snacks

Our stomachs churn walking up the steps
in the laughter of hailing cabs to turn.

I sit in the backseat while Nico & Jux
take on the middle.

The driver takes us to our destination
but all I notice is the bum on Houston
signaling his fingers to a
blazing sun
pouring particles of rays on my face
while a driver speeds through vortex tunnels
before closing my eyes
to lucid lands
sky wide & wise.

But that smiling soul of mine
is always glowing
for the moment
Of all of the above.

Sit//A//Tone-(in//

I'll pace to the ends of subway platforms to get my legs warm with adrenaline.
My headphones push out electricity while I seek a sense of familiarity.
So you take your chance. Shy away. Initiate
until you've got nothing more to say

Deadbeat Boom Box

*I used to treasure all things lost
& choose to aspire volumes
into something found.
I perspire with violins,
feeling difference in classical existence.*

*I've never
shared
the
habit
of sharing
all that
I
truly
care about*

*Scribble Scrabble
in the sweet sheets
of giggled relief.
Riding waves while hiding a peek
of the peaks.*

*I wake up in the arms of an unexpected boy
with a sweet soul,
dabbling in the senselessness
of kidjoythrills.*

*I love articulation
& my thoughts have bombarded themselves in the bubble of
babble*

*I'll come back through
Brilliance & Brightness,
Fueling my sensibility, motivation, & imagination
with a whipped sense of renewal*

Part 2

Lunchbreak smokes with 3 ladies on imperial rooftops,
=
in power & pursuit,
we're all trying to hide our flaws from each other
Mine was the self-imposed prudence of resistance & repetition compulsion

A lover with beauty, grace, intelligence
& genuine intensities.
Is all I care for infusion.

I got the urge to make something matter,
grab what's better,
& stick with flavor

Phrasing things can be tricky in this head of mine.
You see, it on the constant go
& while at times I'm high & might
other times I dibble with babble
For the sake of poking & peeking
at the forces & faces
hiding &seeking
beneath the surface
of structured entity

We are united through moans of unison
in modes of division,
equating to the collaborations
of simplified form.

I'll think of mutuality & am fully aware of its unreachable effect
in the midst of impatience,
desiring union and patience

I've learned you can't dwell on the dream but rather hope for the treat all humbly.
The main part is to take this for all it's worth TODAY & MAKE IT COUNT

Hand In Hand vs. Hungry Ghost Islands

Dirt creeps in skin
smoke dips in sin.
Influential & impressionable
you've got a passion for all the wrong things
that entertain and tame
spots in your brain
killing moments
smooth & smiling
& now I can't help but scratch my recently hair slice
while craving a burger and shower
at 3:39am

I've always floated.
Stumbling into the living dream of prospect in retrospect.

I am hungry and when I feed there is a quench for taste and comfort;
always conquering the stale unsettlement.

Dearest M,
There's a side of me that's been delaying ink on paper for a few days,
restricting a stream of consciousness in a space of vast mindsets

This is a pattern in my lifestyle:
I breathe in. Breathe out
Live fast. Lay low.

I treasure experiences for all that they're worth,
while tiring myself out as I indulge in apathetic distractions,
Taking hold of time in absent addiction.

*Every hit I take burns the barbaric pace of my brain
—all numbness temporary until distress surfaces the inevitable—
yet numbness provides the largest illusion of strength because it dulls the collapse of cornered psyche.*

*Intuition is damaged
when what's imagined
takes full control.*

I restore myself after 40 hour work weeks & rapid living. Making the city my playground for rampant dreaming.

Last night I wanted to kill time by climbing a fence and breaking into my building's swimming pool. I exerted strength and felt accomplished in giving myself the test.

All our lives, I've seen that we could climb trees, fences, and mountains, yet all I had the guts to do was wrap my legs around a sliding pole in skillful descent.

After hopping the fence, I thought of you by my side under a dark lit sky

---

M83 uplifts my senses at the Bowery Ballroom followed by crashing delight with Nico & Star at the Boiler Room. Nico's place keeps me safe while Star stays up with me to watch Ghostbusters. She doesn't want me to meet the man with good hands from Cockbar last week.

I'll gladly listen.

*Sometimes I wonder how close I should get to strangers. I feel this urge to float away from a grounded sense of being, yet remain in a daze for whenever I'm needed. I always feel safe at night when I'm tucked away in the privacy of a peaceful solitude—
Dealing with walking a middle ground in the best and worst of both worlds.*

I'm seeing 2 hairdressers.
One is overbearingly responsive to my existence, while the other is overbearingly unresponsive to his own… let alone mine

We share the commons and opposites of solid truths,
set to consume
like blazed out fools.

Right now I'm only aware that things are not over with this town and him.
&even though I can't rest until resolution sets in

        I'm a kid overloaded with thought
            cuing into clues
        since being six in 1992.

Do unto others what is done onto you. Urbana is nothing more than a chain reaction of repetitive action. I am ignored & in return I will ignore the next person who offers me all they can. I crave an equal and love a challenge but silence is an impulsive trick.

I was attracted to how he floated. A priceless grin and blue round eyes that blink distances while adding to intrigue. He is sad& happy—you can't ever tell.
He floats away from sight while I float into wonder;
 fantasizing of possibility in solitude.

That's how it works.

He told me had a dream the night before where he was still awake and watched the sun come up. He was puzzled in a joyous stupor. We drank away from each other and eventually put our guards down. He gave me a disclaimer about how the process is new to him. He likes me but is not used to it. Also someone else just revealed that they "really" like him. He apologizes for mixed signals & goes on about the process,.

I kiss his cheek& say:
"it's okay"

The rest is history.
We gradually embrace the interlock.
"Everyone gives a fuck when you don't give a fuck"

A Strand in the open web

The dream says:
"Reduce yourself into the eureka of continuity"

I woke up away from the rut
in a handmade world
pouring out the sun,
exiting glimmers of confusion

A cheap distanced disservice
tamed by bum fuck curiosity.

I'm in control.

*Within these clouds, I'm surrounded with great friends
-Igniting delight-
putting a fresh roof over my head.*

*Dream lovers letting me jubilate in silence while seeking
wisdom in rad commission.*

*I am set to consume both taste & bodies.
My mind easily wanders when I have an empty stomach,*

straying from breath.

*I thought of a teacher I don't know & wondered what kind of
stamina he possessed.
I thought of one of his students
-someone I've always wanted to know further-
& imagined the both of them in wall to wall action*

*Total Mentor//Protégé slamdown.
Cute*

Simplicity in the cold nights of New York City.

Rejuvenated by reality
at the stroke of midnight,
I slept in the Boiler Room last night.
Nico, Star & I downing blunts, bowls, and BK.
we watch Surfwise & The Hunger
bidding cheers,
to a first round
of quality living

After poking and prodding some resurfaced thoughts,
I never stayed awake to watch Rivers Edge
& crumbled into sleep for the next 10 hours.

I woke up feeling ready.
The morning sky resembling a sense of twilight.

The coldest day of the year is filled with snow sludge & no sun.
Never knowing who won
Still waters run deep,
with bigger dreams defying compact size.

Silent emotion run through surfaced silence,
in dual opposition
creating the visions
of alienated accomplishment.

I spent the night at Grandma's
she reminded me that blood is thicker than water
& that time doesn't change but people do.

The outside streets leave me feeling like raw bait exposed to the eyes
of hungry scum—whistling at me to devour in disgust.
& despite the odds
I remain uplifted.
Picking up the pace of city space.

Family makes me anticipate to reacquaint
warmth in boundless space.

Bunny took me to a party a couple of nights ago.
Xio was dj'ing & we danced with crowd of bodies to old songs in a free floor. A stranger told me he remembers seeing me around and could never forget my sight. I ask him where we could have met but the music muted out his answer.

Live & Let Live

Star arises from distress. We smoked a blunt at the boiler room and ate Chinese in Houston. Speaking of friendships and the quality of bonds with the lost or found.
Walking in the mist of lower east side humidity
while she leads the way & looks over at my scattered pace.
We took the train back home and ended up going our separate ways until next time.

Live and Let live
Was the moral of dinner with Grandma yesterday.
History repeats itself and solitude is a feared destiny
some of us sacrifice our dignity for to avoid.

I'm learning the best that I can with the most that I have.
It's not even about less or more
but rather how to grow form.

Beat the Devil

Shilpa sings about her dreams in Albuquerque,
& I sit on Nick & Eddie's couch while they switch to older tunes,
preaching about magic & loving it so.

Could it be magic?

The gathering of sweetness,
sliding not colliding,
beneath the skin of fascination.

Eager & hungry minds
Ignite delight
when sparking beauties incite
charms, luck & love

in the memory locks
of a heart shaped drop.

We reminisce on phase
by creating a present
of equal days
devouring comfort food phase.

Bowing our head to the hands of better dreams,
holding your cigarette to the burn of melting chemicals
from a paper tree,
& the plush glow of smoke soaks
within earthly roots.

We were born to dream
to win or lose
the suckers game
of good calls
& better times.

Dream Warrior

"

At the sight of night
reliving the bright exposures of the sun.

At the sight of 2 birds
soaring high in the branches above singing in lyrical chirps:

"fortunes are never quiet"

I wonder if I've revealed too much of myself
& what I have revealed of myself.
I think of warm-ups and linger my limbs loose against the dark
dashboard of night & vehicle.

"Forget your tears // forget your mind // forget yourself//
But remember me"

I'm teased by breeze & fucked by west coast breeze
ripping through holes
of designer jeans.

This is the beginning of the end.

Trauma Sucks.

My skin moves to fuck its disdain
I breathe in. I breathe out
& rise to the fence ahead

Vehicles shift styles
In destination & obligation

I have places to go
& this is all mine

I, thing

I think of the mix I made & never gave. I gave it a good listen earlier.
It plays & skips with zip scratches
of cock sucking first love

Highway cities are composed of corporate pit stops,
Surveilling commodity and convenience.

I fill the car with gasoline and try to charge it. The machine asks for my zip code & then instructs "please see attendant" She is jolly but preoccupied at the phone and says the card won't go through.
I give her cash and piss in the shady bathrooms

No one can track with cash
Sitting on the rocks of Venice Beach.

Nothing beats this.

Happy Birthday Star,
I had a dream that old things become reborn
& there is nothing wrong with celebrating it new form.

The love we've encountered in others have taught us the hard luck love lessons
for a better tomorrow.

The good may grieve
but they don't suffer.

I feel refined out here
Beginning to the end

// The consolidation of people builds up inside your being //

I'm hitting the road again.

// They intrude inside you but hide from you //
// why should others bear sympathy towards you if you barely got it for yourself? //

I'm on the steps of steep hills overlooking the damned streets of Broadway, San Fransisco. Brick ovens burn away the nutrients to bring a taste that compounds your insides. I pampered myself to the brim of expenses but we'll work ourselves away when we return from vaycay.

I've got an urge to blend with chance and opportunity.
None of my roots have ever been paved smoothly,
but their strands are what made the paradise

The clarity of intention marvels interaction.

I look downhill and I see a man playing guitar,
gearing toward hopelessness with the power of strings

The homes get pink with sunlight up ahead. Behind the fence an olive house with black and red trimmings mark the start of a new road.
A clean glimmer strips across its barrier representing the sole promise to must always give yourself:

Survive duality
with others // in yourself

The 2 birds sing their songs in the burst red explosion of sun and sky.

In the end we all seem to want to bring it down toward a level of sheer awareness and brisk articulation. I'm watching music videos in the Boiler Room, looking for absolute focus in the freezing moments. I have nothing more do but live in proper flow—

-DEFYING DOLLHOOD FRENZY-

(My bones are the gears which motion me forward)

Everything seems out of sight // out of mind
The Waking world grants me thought
of prime connection thriving in reciprocation
The sounds of admiration speaking through the barriers of silence,
is a melody worth listening to.

Nightmares are untouched ravagings
That tease with depravity.

I'll open my eyes,
glowing yellow grays.

The wind howls in the morning
with lukewarm brushes of wind
clouding toward or away from you.

(it always depends which way you're going)

I-86 Diner

Preservation is the spare piece that gives away time.
& this place is visually cozy with it's baby, pink, & blue contrast

The sun blasts on my face
building up its rays,
for a warmth that closes my eyes in imaginary state.

While Rochester is a cold, dark haven for some,
I burst into it with a sense of adventure.

I've come to learn that festering in eagerness is what causes backfire
& I'm through with exhausting myself backwards

There is no reason to surrender
nor is there a reason to withhold away from selling yourself short.

Anxiety is an enemy of bleak vision irrationality
awakening to redefine the enemy.
It ticks away seconds from your time
until it's fueled with petty distractions
& stolen value.

Chance unravels
showing you and proving it wrong

But anxiety festers all the possibilities
until it manifests
in smoky fulfillment
of being victim & pray
to the chase of a game.

Chance is the flickering star
untouched by angst.

I take a train to Grandma's and the idea of being inside the train horrifies me after a couple of stops. Everyone was glued to the games on their iPods. Some put the volumes of their beats, looking at the person next to them and nodding in agreement.

Another man was also fixated on the gaze of his game. The 5 people across from me are plugged into their pod machines— sinking into brief sleep or blink blank visions

A private audio that helps us function in motional nothingness.

I hear the chattering of coins & slamming shouts of sliding doors.
A legless man shakes his cup of change
&only speaks in gratitude.
for the clinking charities he is bound to.
He makes his way to the next set of sliding doors.
-SILENCE-

There was a man across from me so fixated on his gaze
that he punched instead of touched
his machine seeking victory.

The train stop & he gets up
yelling at the still sliding doors
"OPEN UP!!!!!"

The ideal is dead
& irritable

Extreme & Lucid

"Victory seeks an embodiment"
"Double standards trap one into temperament"
"The trick is to cultivate goodness"

*Basking under the sun, I feel the urge to stir away the hard
grips of current challenge
through thick skin.*

*Nothing is so strange,
as waiting in the winds
before walking on stage*

*I am testing the limits of your nerves
since mine shake like they do.*

*Our nerves transcend from fear to bliss
-in common urge to attain ability-
Fucking our limits one step at a time.*

*The extreme body is only limited by
competing captivations of
spectator spectrums.*

*BDD is the visual effect of bodily distortion
never amounting to an embodied sense of ful-fill-ment.*

*FUCK BODY DYSMORPIC DISORDER.
It is the embodiment of bullshit,
birthed from your taste of the ideal gaze
searching through mindful holes
in your brain*

There is an alchemical precept that states:
"Through repetition the magic will be forced to rise"

Timeless

To overcome otherness we must learn to see the essence of self in others **(interbeing)**
It is possible to experience a deep understanding of the universe when we expand personal insights into cosmic experience

Choose your side // Never a Side

the ideal is dead

Essence & radiance

glimmer fluidity.

Momentum comes with discipline,
able to quiet the mind.
Spontaneity does not translate to chaos,
though it's surely not exempt from it.
"My body is like a lighting rod"
in constant wonder of what will come.
To & From (**gazepost**)

The dominance of mind brings the absence of the heart.
Desire comes in so many shapes, that it shifts from being and location.
When we realize the potency of thought, we understand the value of purifying it.

To relish in confession & transcendence, we must ditch the pressures of trial & error.
Once we are made aware of our tightness & uptightness
We can begin to release inner essence
as a common thread to connect

I'm awake.
Banned by priorities
,late home entrances,
& artificial stimulation
granting edge with awareness.

I communicate with ease & absorb the impulses of dazed action.

Life gets in the way when varieties leave their mark as plates on the table,
showing off your needs and desires. I continue to be stripped of ideas & insight in the wake of tragic loss. Yet even in the sheering gaze of her life slipping away she silently assures me that there's no excuses & to not over exert myself at the brim of damaged doubts. She knows it'll take rounds of compulsion before I truly get it but in the end it's all about resurfacing hope beyond the distance of better tomorrows.

Tell the World

Craving to bring it all down
in awareness & articulation.

Moving trains shake the body into a dollhood frenzy of crucial destination

Do we embrace the surges of struggle or the splashes of splendor?

Knowledge is tamed by damage
in the hysterical truths of expression
rooted in past experience.

I saw M83 with Star & Xio last night.
The sound was incredible despite the crowd

In rare moments did I smile at a stranger, talk to other ones, & tell an annoying one to quit smacking my ass and not be shy to speak.

My wisdom teeth are coming in—
tapping into prime exclusion
while wondering the significance of whatever gaps.

Control over a numb solution is insignificant.

Out of sight // out of mind

Otherly

I'm watching music videos,
warm in the boiler room sweetness;
hunting for absolute focus in the midst of senseless observation.

I have nothing more to do but live & have it work with me.

The waking world grants me thought.
It's only through prime connection that we may thrive in
reciprocation.

The sounds of admiration
speaking through the barriers of silence
is a melody worth listening to

Untouched
& teased by hunger
I open my eyes to a brand new day
Glowing in yellow shade.

The wind howls with lukewarm brushes,
clouds moving toward
or away from you
(because it always depends on which direction you're going)

My bones are the gear which move me forward
The funny part is I don't know where to start
or when to stop.

I've come to realize how in the past 5 years, I've been safe through the shelter of others. This was never intended. I just seek. Can being blessed come out of luck? I don't know but it works for me & I've made sure to do what I can to make it work for them.

I'm seeking the proper motions of interaction guiding to a pretty piece of flesh
willing to give & take
at the same pace.

Locked in gaze, I'll always wonder
"is there anything wrong with redundant pleasure?"

The Hope lounge was the place to be for a last minute appearance, Ariel taking Nico & I for some after party treats.

All I ask for is a dose of Absolut quality I will gladly see
for equilibrium simplicity in a crowd of strangers & happenings
the boiler room beauty shelter helps me breathe into the next day

<u>West Side Youthery</u>

I walk through West 4th & wait for a train to take me somewhere I've never been too.

I make my own space front row at the latest show,
taking a few hit to heart,
assuring my luck boy charms:
joy will follow you
in solitude.

Purify your emotions // while always toasting to the motion
burning in the back of your mind.

I wait for another train & cure my ears from live sound
& danced limbs of my psyche
resurfacing away
psychic pins,
craving to be catered too

in constant fear of expired treat,
barely focused on the main course.

I-86 DINER.

This place is cozy to the eyes.
Baby pink & blue fuzz.

It's so quick to strip your bliss once you've attained it. The sun blasts on my face building up its rays for a warmth that closes my eyes towards a hazy reality. While Rochester is a cold, dark haven for some, I burst into it with grace & ease.

The shattered eagerness of possibilities creates the backfire
I'm through it.
There is no reason to surrender nor is there reason to withhold

"you've gotta take it as it comes" -Vivian Girls

The anxious enemy creeps irrationality into the waking moment—intruding bleakness in possibility. It ticks away seconds from your time until fueled by distractions which rob it of it's value.

Chance unravels
Showing you
& proving it wrong

But anxiety festers all the possibilities until it manifests into a smoky fulfillment
of being the victim //pray // chase // of the game.

To seek & redeem we are consumed by the irrelevant streaks of downtime luck before the fall.

Bunnyville sagesesh

Victory seeks an embodiment
imitating audio // visual compliment.

Bunnies pour the smoke of good vibes & fresh starts.
Blowing out the sparks of deep red candles
// wishing the best //

"To love & be loved"

Irrationality quickens the pace & decay of future days;
Fervors of idiocy distracting us from priority.

We want the chance to breathe away from states any states of mind
that don't coincide.

I feel like this is the silence before a bloom—
BOOM
All barriers awaken.

& you become smothered by paradise.

Do you care about it when it crumbles in your face?
For one reason or the other you have no idea what to expect

Except that you want out from this bubble of idiocy
You want out from the inconvenience
of a lack of comfort.

Our main incentive is to adopt any form of wellness
dictated by notions of
dis-ease

Like all other forms of thought
we loan our bodies
To the dominant and submissive structures of our gaze

Surrounded in the openness of institutional architecture—

I dream of swallowing solution, manifest into physicality & drive
away from the bubble
of kindred opposition

I accomplish tasks
errands
& early morning social gatherings
-to compensate for the night before-
& the strange feeling that plunges into your psyche when surrounded by
impenetrable importance.

I seek to drain my shell & shed some habits to create better ones.

I'm digging through my skin
in the warm weather blaze
of displaced defense

Last night all the ones I negated stared me straight in the eye
Tonight that side will disappear

MayDay

I'm in an airplane going back & forth between sweet sedation & anxious awareness—reminiscing on the lost possibility.

Now I read about Philip K. Dicks neurotic pre cogs
(people who can dip into the future & have empty recollections of the past)

This trip came during a turbulent time with finals but the beautiful space of family & west coast breeze helps me structure recent epiphanies.

EXPLOSIVE // INTRUSION.

These are the ramifications of personal anxiety—a hyperawareness bouncing to the other side of delight. I'm fixated in doubt & the rush of it is equivalent to surges of manic thrill
casting a glow

Lumber-gaze

It's ironic how in my desire toward him, I make sheer discoveries about myself.

My stranger on the train helped me realize what I was worth the other day.

What are the rest afraid of?
Guarded with closed comfort & insincere welcomings
waiting to be challenged, confronted, & relinquished.

Dynamo

Process brings elimination & liberation.
I write with the view of houses on hilltops while
Alcest screams *Elevation* to my ears.

I'm given life & therefore breathe experience into my life because I could never deal with the shellshock of being stuck in stagnation. So I dissect my vision into a tale worth

telling, showing, & being

2 of cups

When I say
THE IDEAL IS DEAD

Elle says:
"Just because something is possible does not mean will happen"

Controlling the outcome of a chance is a power worth tapping into
The wind blows decent recognitions of things that have been & will be.

I'm sliding into victory & quality mindfulness. This has been a rough chapter but it ends soaring with survival.

Limits only exist to preserve current embodiment.
// Transcend outlook to manifest outcome //

Intensity is a flavor worth possessing.
Stand your ground
& choose your side //
Never a side

2 birds settle on the bare branches ahead of me,
intertwining mid-air momentarily.

One flies away while the other stands strong.

I've got rush of time by my side.
Imaginations all mine
twinkling hope through prosperity's dime.

So much to go for
Never settling for less.

The branch is bare.

Absinthe in the Airplane

I drink some with Grandma.
We reflect of life, death, & traumas,
Knowing well there is no other choice but living with all you can
& passing through the dead ideal
with a quality alternative set to enhance.

Dear Synchronicity,
Ready, Set, Glow
I'm above your dawn tinted clouds & bright moon;
Delivering a wide smile

Ready to Go.

Run Down (maybe link it to other story about the train?)

A woman in white comes into a train.
She has rosary beads hanging off her bag
& begins to beg.

I give her a dollar, notice the scabs in her arm
& let grim thoughts form in my mind.

She digs through the folded pile of dollar bills while a big man looks over her shoulder. They laugh and snort empty victories of being drunk on junk. She never says thank you for the dollar, smirks in the midst of strangers, & gets onto another train to start her game all over again.

Bums approach the train
wishing for hope
pleading with purpose
decayed by destiny.

Frisbees in Utopia

Thin sheer sweaters shine white in the wind.

We claim our bodies to boundary
bringing boredom
helping us define the structure behind
scattered origins.

Anxiety recognizes when it loses control of control

This is primal.

There was something in the company of bunnies that welcomed the company of wolves.
I have no idea why these things happened, but we left our Bunnyville mourning the dead ideals—going up north, headed to the city, staying in the dead zone.

Our best bet was to stand with grace
& stray from the melting wax
of steamed disappointment,

The answer is always right in front of you but sometimes all it takes is a little revision.
I've rushed through experiences and relations in quicker ways than others
to avoid confrontation.

It always follows you though
the ghosts of memories
you leave behind
linger in the shape of golden ideals
until you answer them in cold truths.

I'm sensitive to something that makes me drown in emotion.
I'm sensitive to the deprivation of experience
even if it's all worth a pile of shit.

I lack a proper sense of timing for fear of losing flexibility.

This is the fluidity that both advances and destroys me.

So now I crave structure & abundance
in both purpose & interaction.

Childs Play

Imagine having thrill as your security blanket.

You spend your childhood sheltered from social interactions until the weekend.
You develop a sense of self based on the spectacles of your imagination

T.V.
& what you see in the city streets

Retreat and sway
to the fusion of musical exposure.

An active imagination while inactive from the interaction.

& then
as you become efficient in mobility
you resist from the boundaries of boring structure.

Being warm in Bunnyville reminds me that I'm never left out in the cold. Sometimes you have to feel the chill before you head to shelter. Disillusioned and righteously resentful, I'm homeless by choice yet never left stranded.
Even in shameful shambles it means the world to have my bunnies assure me in security. I'm running from a figure unseen

in the chase between rapid motion & edged darkness,
something's always gotta give.

What lays underneath the bleak empty shapes of slashed pursuit,
sitting comfortably in your psyche?

Jux says I'm a soldier when it comes to conquering the blur.
Last night we became lost boys & intoxicated our nerves
away from sobering doubt.

He looks at me & asks
"what are you thinking?"

I think about the chase
& reflect on the existent threads
of constant possibility
creating a conclusion
that hasn't even seen the light of day.

I'll articulate anxieties when I have zip fear from you knowing that
You don't deserve
Heaven
You are it.
& the idea of ashing my skin
In the shape of one
Forever
Remembered as a Star

Star interludes

To achieve intention you must eliminate expectation

"You know the answer Dear One?
So why do you choose to transcend toward nothing more than suffering?
You know how to predict whatever your desires,
So do yourself a favor little brother & don't cheat yourself of fresh starts by
dwelling on a dragged past. Escape becoming trapped by the unborn opportunity
so that you can embrace it at it's birth."

The Quality of character is the only necessity to get by

It's been raining streams almost every day.
I'm inside a Starbucks with Star
waiting for a movie to start in an hour.

My optimism is restless
but my ideals have been touched by the shade of jaded recovery //

I long for contact with quality.
A fresh face that I can adore // a fresh connect worth speaking for.
I long for a different kind of affection.
A beautifully honest challenge

Not shy of reciprocation & sparked interaction

Someone new.

Secret Garden

"We all hide & seek"

The secret is teamwork
Give me something better // spare me something worse

The paradise of knowledge is contained by capability.

Those with visible defects
hide in the fear of understanding
while those that understand don't bite fear

The most fruitful grounds are the ones pasted by past growth.
A soul floats in the evolving pastures of rubbled gardens paved for reconstruction.

PART 2

Lara phrased it right last night:
"THE FREAKS ARE OUT"

I finally got my own place last night:
big boy making big moves

A part of me is anxious—conscious over fresh liberty and unseen struggle.
Diminished doubts are nothing more than particles of dust,
floating as an existent entity
But touching nothing

Ricochet and I spent the day in Coney.
We kissed on the beach & rode The Cyclone

I took it for what it was
knowing that we got the chemistry down but not the connection.

If it's one thing I learned from that sour mouthfuck,
it's that immediate gratification
dulls the richness
of both patience & interaction.

I'm moving to a new place & once again find an urgency to run as a new found figure
filled with upgraded ripe & insatiable spice.
If you cannot fathom taste
but are an object to someone else's,
the best thing you can do is learn & run.

Living in the Labyrinth won't hit me until it's actually happened.

Wasted days are crimes of doubt // leaving us shaken // all around // multiple sound

Escapism is my habit
in the shadows of a doubt

The music plays & each face screened on the projector tells a story
with a blank stare.
Lara and I are surrounded by elders
who blink & chew the appetites of time.

We grin a teenage lightening
of daring eyes & darling speed.

Shine my Superstar
for you are all I see.
We are alive with the repetition of done deeds & bad habits
dying hard

Blood is thicker than water // Soul is thicker than blood

I seek to rid myself of damaged compulsion // pointless in motion
// in stunted notion.

I turned off the light and sound,
to close my eyes and tune to the noise
of cars speeding through the night in a highway that never sleeps.

I'm having trouble breathing properly
& lose track due to thought:
SO MUCH THOUGHT!

Crumbling through my head
in eye opening darkness
staying still.

I assume that maybe this is all part of the perk
for being in a better place.

The next day I secretly wonder,
in a stream of sink dream clutter—

Is legitimation only delivered by validation?
& is it really that simple?

I got these new headphones to block out the sounds of silence.

I'm being a baby.

Stuck in fervors of disenchantment,
when in all actuality I have it made in ways that are easier for some
& challenging for others.
Perceptions are boundless in the current boundary of coordinated
being.
The experience is what we long for
& it has been manifested
the ignition of fruition

craving to flourish from the animated cocoons of dead cells & shedded skin.

We breathe a flavor of unique taste, arising from the different tracks of existence.
We dance with simplicity while indulging with fine

Sense	sounds	sights
Stories	style	scents

-company is bliss-
while associations determine the better half

We breathed in the safety of our sanctuaries:
busses // cars // trains // crowded streets // the homes of our mothers, fathers, & lovers// The Boiler Room // Bunnyville // The Dream Pad // The labyrinth // the cabin.

Impatience & Anxiety stir in me like laced ingredients in a sweet dish

& yet I no longer decide to bond over miseries & assumptions. Maybe it's my attempt to glimmer the contemplations with a worthwhile shine. I want to transcend the experience from warrior to mastery & turn all foreign elements into acquainted ones.

I feel divided from my experience. As if I took steps toward them without entrance. Perhaps it's only a matter of time before whatever quality elation hits again.

I'm ready to be fulfilled.

Not in tainted artificial ways but in the pure style of

head, heart & soul

There are roots rising to fruition but it all seems to be something unknown for something felt before.

The burn of whatever burdens is impermanent.

Williamsburg happenings force away any ounce of darkness that once corrupted its streets.
We see trends manifest always testing the value of one thing or another.
Pan

How do you explain intention while in tension?

I watch him read
& desire floats over our heads
undefined, undeclared,
up in the air
like a pack of colors
admired from a distance.

Separate from form
because we are both scattered souls,
seeking a quality that is visible to us
yet transparent & fleeting inside of us.

Healers & Renegades
running from a pack of vicious cycles
& disappointment.

Yet here I am,
always bringing a hungry mind seeking to
connect, construct, & create

all fantasies into a reality.

& whether I acknowledge or comprehend such intentions
as an attempt to magnify the chance of immediate gratification—

My desire to blend is always there.
Should I resent it? Ignore it? Welcome it as something natural?

I've always been so committed to the intent that bind pieces of myself in states of boundlessness.

I'm releasing a stage of rage that periodically comes my way.
The WORST you can do is fester & foster the tensions inside of you.

Naïve

I slept a full 9 hours while tossing and turning my way into it.
My father once told me that when you fall asleep with your hand in your heart,
Nightmares will come.

I did just & filled myself with so much.
Seeds of doubt dispersing my pillow.

I welcome the bad dreams & dare them to take me into the next level.
All they manage to do is wake me up feeling angry & alive.
Simply meditating to ease my psyche back to the surface.

Just because the nightmares come doesn't mean they stay right?

Runaway

I refrain from practice because the stagnating rush of escaping into myself is a bad habit that leads to nowhere.

What makes staying still any different?
My thoughts scan memories attempting to decode recent days passed while
Feeling free yesterday
& tense today.

Absent stability is a scary thought,
marked by whatever isolated figure I appear to be.

I'm in states of disarray because I feel weight
down
by tra // u // ma
By ex // per// I// ence
By solitude
By whatever company surrounding me
By absorption
making me feel fucking nauseous.

This is nothing new to me
& all I find myself doing is absorbing
in experience
in isolation
inter active

I walked ahead of the crowd yesterday & Merrick called me out on my good energy

Burning Up

I think respect is crucial.
Mastery... servitude... it's all an extreme illusion we conduct
ourselves with in order to stay entitled or shed our spirit in the splits
of extreme escape.

With escape comes the full rush of desiring, extending, & pushing the
weights of paced experience.

The other night I attempted to conquer my fear of the cold by laying
down next to him in snow covered grounds,
hoping for the heat of bodies to turn us all around.

The rest of the night was nothing more than memories of a
bittersweet constellation, claiming we'd get to our destination faster
by letting false wishing loose.

I bounced & asked him to navigate...

I had to welcome whatever
pace there laid
in having him look at my world.

Star always affirms their worth to me underground
& dudes like him provide only a static sound
unworthy of being bound.

& yet I'm haunted by the gallow whispers of another man
sucking & hanging
accelerating his mouth
for a sense of reward
to the question
"does truth bow to beauty or does beauty bow to truth?"

"They gave you a heart // you gave them a name"

The truth is he led me on with an ego more transparent than the clouding of false desires,

Strength in stress
Seeks validation with a lack of ammunition

Dumped without touch,
A dream boy destroyed
scattering my mind in past dust
with pieces hightailing a known path
of fresh chance paved
through shifting shapes
released & immersed
by an imagination
teased by the worst.

Scared >> ambitious >> tense >> cold,
I make my way through the crowd
& get served drinks
while staring out the windows
of grand heights reaching higher status.

Alex Niki hugs me tight,
acknowledging the turbulent flourishings of change,
assuring me of a solid spot whenever I was ready

Page Explain

                        The future is unborn
                    Maybe a part of me can
                            sense it
                            dream it
                            be it

                  I envision it burning into the past
                    folding over into a clean slate
                                  & fresh velocity

Yet I'm floating in a haze of dreams, reality, & the perception or both.
& know that I cannot be stuck in such states of seeing.

I need to move >> manifest
but when? How?
Shall I float into a moment that unfolds?

It's been done before... gotta score some faith

                    By converting our emotions are we in denial of suffering?
                        or are we simply evolving toward peaceful progression?

The pages are at the point where we once again mention the closing chapter of our adventure.

                    We admire the coincidence // We run toward destination
// We ignore & dodge the obstacle but only can as fast as missing our boarding //

We have an extra hour of time of time by our side.
How will we spend it?
Sitting down at the empty gate waiting for our next ride?

Cruising our thoughts from pen to paper?
Failing this moment to accomplish the next one?

Sugar Hiccup

**Every breath brings change
for what is done will be undone to yet another
gone thing**
    We become scared of losing our comfort because of intoxicating condition.

It hasn't rained this hard in a while. There is something. There is something tranquil and sedating about everything taking place.

I meditate >> Write >> exercise >> eat >> sleep
& go to a friends for a lovely homemade dinner
while the sounds of multiple drops
crash on the window

Giddy Edge of Light

I cruised through in pleasant frequency & collective effervescence of a Miss Jo protest

Proud of my friend's accomplishment, I detach from the crowd &
walk a private path
of wide open skies
birds soaring circular
over high,

"through the winters woods"
I think about the distance I inflict for a peace of mind

releasing tense uncertainties
I think of how we contain energies
kinetic
toward conscious connections

Reserved, preserved, & knotted
in the secure substance // sustenance
Of fewer souls spotted
In the fogs of wish fulfillment

Where am I? I'm in the present moment?

Precise Illumination

The sun sets a lavender glow
twisted within the strands
of intertwined worlds.

The sounds of water streaming from the faucet is a crystal clear
comparison
between beautiful scene
& toxic stream

Today was the first day of warmth

God Eat God

Confusion distorts
denials disguise
In the picture perfect imagery
of scenery absent from harm.

I sit with Dani in a space along the Hudson river—
A tainted body composed with waste.

A BEAUTIFUL DUMP
radiated by the sun
shining the sky
Blue & Clear

Danielle's girl is shriveled in a frenzy of lashing anxiety
Isolating visible charms.

Waiting to be recovered by touches
of candy & weed.

The soul of a child // in the body of a woman.

She breathed impatience
& bathed in the dizzying sights
of intention
I could relate to her on gripping tight

Whatever is dear
Before form
Flourishes near.

Something feels different,
familiar in clarity
but further from recognition.

We were in the streets
where my soul begun the streams
of endless city bus rides
& adrenaline fused car rides

BEAMS OF EXPERIENCE

Absorbed >> relished >> & taken for granted
In the collapse of absent desires
& self-avoidance,
Because the only thing I could think about was escaping this moment
To pursue finer ones.

& I did.

I saw everything I was capable of behind the screens of my eyes.
Dreaming the distress of constant goals met

allowing me to float
in & out
of consciousness

Conditions are temporary & while we cringe at its intrusion
                    we ironically blend within its nest.

We self-destruct when we shoot away our senses to the total rapture
of a trap
                    whether it feels good or bad.

It's not about being ahead of the game more-so than being at the right place at the right time. I'm staring at the back doorway of Fanellis café. The waitresses operate rapidly to provide the right kinds of service.
We all seem trapped in our heads today… Letting overcast emotion creep over our skulls with fear & anticipation. If you were look at the person you are today >> years down the line >> would you turn away blindly looking for the next safe fix or would you smile at the being that brought you there with every ounce of intensity & tenderness that fueled the days it once breathed.

To escape into experience consciously only takes you so far.
Mindless interaction is as clouding as the pits of solitude
We're all destined for.

                      A prelude to the core

I sit on branches & absorb the heat
                              breeze
                                   & sounds of music.
                    in the heat of a hunted stream
   while "Genie's Drugs" sucks out my lucky charm.

"Nobody takes you like you do"

I put my hands out,
in the midst of dancing nerves
ready to run,
Spread wide for the sun

After days of rain & battling the idea of solitude over celebration, I am letting the day take me by storm. Oveglazed by a bittersweet // sweetbitter Summer set to teach a lesson of spiritual hardknocks.

My body races through the city streets to discover sensation. Wisdom is exhausting because it grants a thirst that remains unquenchable.
I feel more than others or myself realize at times. Star helps me appreciate depth.
She shows me how to embrace it in genuine beauty without shame. We dream to see the details of our path in chariot seats with glistening skies overhead.

Existent in terms of being perceived & experienced.
Distracted in ways that turn your head from the details of a current moment.

The power of being Lost & Found

You take your time alone, anticipating the company that will stream along in flow.

Strangers, who are you?

& why am I fixated by your stories to tell a part of mine?

Stagnation rushes into foolishness, a quality that we portray in ultimate visibility, inspired by twinkled experience. You have the choice to let it all fall free from brackets of division.

Spread yourself across to the best of both world because this moment
right here // right now
will bring you everything that it's worth.

Oh, but the urge!

Of experiencing all possibilities. & the dwelling surges of leaving them untouched.

what do I do?
How do I do?

But don't you realize this is your time?
Right here? Right now?
Your impatience and search for thirst will drain you quicker than you are able to experience any joy to come along your way. You have the power to make it happen.

IGNORE PAST INJUSTICE.

because you have learned, flourished, & experienced the rare treat of transcending capacity imposed on you for a better sense of being.

You will make it happen.
Because each page proves that you already have

WE ARE WITH YOU DEAR ONE

When a key breaks how do you fix it?
Learn & make your knowledge both capable and concrete

Arise your roots

& DISSOLVE TO RESOLVE

Clarity breezes through our body & mind at the peaks of discovery
& disintegrates at the sight of disappointment
// the loss of mindfulness

As the lights of memory flash through your decision
your only choice is to extend patience

ELIMINATING PANIC CONTROL

Your language determines your victory but your silence speaks louder than words

A bus passes & I watch it stop forward
// eagerly awaiting to climb into another story //

> *Be patient Dear one,*
> *I'm with you for life.*
> *Tragic is as tragic does.*
> *but stick close to the quality*
> *& you won't stray from cosmic path*

> *Together & Divided*
> *I'll always love you*

Flavor of the Day.

The other night I had to do fieldwork at a leather bar as the last straw and final perk.

Lj & Baby Greta convinced me that it was in my best interest
& so I venture to the city alone,
becoming in tune with synchronicity.

I run into Aunt Tim at the train station & we catch up on our pre party locations:
He's headed to a place called Monster // I'm headed to the Gorillaz album release party.

It was an underground happening,
leaving my bunnies & me as innocent bystanders
in an "exclusive" mix of
hipsters, grubs, shrubs,
in grand center appeal.

The music didn't fuel me much, because my head only pulsated a clock to research.

After going our separate ways I meet Aunt Tim at the Monster—a cute place that's well lit on the outside with a 50s diner appeal, only instead of booths there was a huge oval bar with stools surrounding it. Aunt Tim brings me to a basement where there's about a dozen men scattered throughout. He introduces me to his friend Ray, a tall, friendly, and devious dude, who looks like a rainbow blasting from rockhard terrain. His speech was slurred and redundant, constantly saying "Hello?" or "WHAT DID I DO!?", in which I would laughingly reply "nothing", & he would say "EXACTLY." He kissed my hand and somehow got me to caress his bald head.

The other 2 men were a Puerto Rican couple who kissed my cheeks at the same time.
They were real nice but disappeared to fight outside.

The DJ was a cute girl around my age. She was real tight with Aunt Tim and even sported a shirt he made for her

Aunt Tim is so sweet.

We went with Ray & hailed cab to The Eagle.
Ray got funny, shameless and redundant again,
& all I thought about was how much of myself I put out there.
"I like your energy" he says, "Don't worry, I'm not a bad guy."

That's what they all say.

I put a wall between us & enjoy the rest of my night at the leather bar.

Looking at the crowd, I scoped men of all shapes and sizes devour desire to quench the hunger. A handsome man pursued me in debaucheries grace & took me to a stall to show me his all.

The man became too busy being insecure
& comparing his inadequacies to my youth.
"Come home with me, so I can fuck you," he whispers in doubtful ecstasy
"Thanks, but no thanks," I say.

That's how it always works with them.

I leave him at the stall with his all standing tall,
jetting the bar to walk the streets of New York alone & aware.

The bums crawled in despair
& I helped one out with a couple of bucks wishing him well.

I followed my lure & ended up at a diner,
exhausted by the refusal to fall asleep.
I read the *4 agreements* & wrote on a napkin:

KMFDM reminds me that I'm naïve:
// THAT'S THE WAY OF THE WORLD // TELL ME
SECRETS
TELL ME SWEET SECRETS
WHAT DO YOU KNOW

WHAT DO YOU KNOW
WHAT DO YOU KNOW ABOUT ME
TAKE ME TO THE OTHER SIDE
WALK THE LINE
THAT'S THE WAY OF THE WORLD
WHAT U WAITIN' 4
SHE HAS TO BE LOVED
EVERYBODY NEEDS SOMEBODY //

I read & write in phases of post-indust glory leaving me in the dust of still pace lacing me toward incomplete boredoms. Where's the effervescence? Where's any essence?
I know this can't be my final destiny… yet all I feel is that nocturnal sense of shame that lingers within my name. I gotta be strong & dip out of eye-roll wrong.

I leave the diner & cruise midtown
in the middle of the night to make it on time for my latest train home. I run into Kate Flowers, & awaken at the sight of her genuine glisten. We catch up & she tells me to be safe. I guess she could see the exhaust from a grace glowing miles away. I hug her goodnight & bounce on the train to make it home before the sun comes up.

3/6/10 >>> 461

Dear sis
Star,
Comes through at midnight.

We catch up and heal our souls in the warmth of genuine love.

We awake to walk in the haze of a beautiful day only to go out separate with an octane sense of faith. I walk back home and my iPod dies mid-way & begin to focus on each breath and step in simplistic attempt to concentrate.

I clean my car for the first time in months
& get rid of a toy frog the blue eyed boogeyman gave my mom.
He's a bastard gone,
in the scraps of disposed memory.

Under

I ask myself
"what is your dream"
While immersed in the wholesome presence of the Maryknoll sisters,
responding to the ambitions & experiences
of my dreams

There is nothing to fear but fear itself.
Whoever said that was so right.
The cold weather struck again & this means nothing aside from old thoughts resurfacing.

Vast & Formless.

At times, I make the mistake if assuming the worst & being outspoken about it.
All of it are old types of seeds expanding on fresh pastures that still have enough space to not be composed to waste.

Where is the rush?? What is the rush??
& why the rush?

Meditation is crucial during times like this but the countdown of a new chapter is nerve-wracking.

I imagine the richest beings in the world & see how boredom is applied to their treasure. I'm on the couch, against the labyrinth's window, allowing great sight.

I'm boundless yet bound by the impact of thoughts & dreams that I cannot disclose with everyone or anyone. It's so easy to become trapped in the mindsets of
Obligation // expectation // & contemplation

Why the urgency?
I'm straying from any sense of priority,
-Indifferent-
& d
    e
      l
        i
          g
            h
              t
                fully apathetic.

No care in the world. How awful & how free.

Pure Erupt

I've tapped into tension at the labyrinth homebase.
The peace is kept & stabilized
but the pressures of tolerable interactions
always reaches a limit
when you gotta escape
or eradicate
in order to eliminate
the desire to instigate
a sting tied rivalry
filled with empty challenge & wasted energy,
resisting celebration.

Neutrality is only saved from aggravation when it's translation
doesn't determine denial in aggravated avoidance.

How does hiding from conflict allow you to notice enough of to make a change? I'm not interested in feeling pain but it is here & it will pass.

Once defined or disguised
in the form of better things to come.

The world is not about pain or joy
but it forces the two to join
in the communicated phases of
Vibration >> connection >> immersion.

Crust Crown

Dust frown // Drown doubt
In the layers your light resides
through rites to shine
& just be fine

Drinking water is supposed to nourish you.

Allow the flow
to drain the past
& breathe into the grip
of the current moment.

Attempt to suppose
Rather than oppose
a peaceful drag
smoking streams
in the flowers of your soul.

Honor your crossroads to intersect & intertwine
prestige in desire.

I'll be embracing joy
by escaping doubts of choice
in the exclusive detail of raw impact
ready to lock & loud
the conclusive contact
Of electric explosion

In the gathered implosions
of lathered fusion.

Perpetual

THE PROCESS MUST FUEL YOU TO NOT STUNT YOU.
The weight of workloads and deadlines must be met.
Fried & Fine,
I have much to say
& more syntax to apply

I worked out smoke free & felt good to be in a sobering stream of peace,
taking all impacts with ease without fixated breeze.

As soon as anxieties attempt to wake me from my slumber,
I remind myself that today will be all that it can be.

"In the BackSeat"

I'm always on this everlasting quest for reassuring discoveries
Maybe I've had it the whole time… or maybe I yearn for it because I don't have it on the inside?

I'm relaxed, pondering, & safe.
No attachments.
No responsibilities.
These are the true desires of lost boy fathom.

Things are most certainly unraveling
& could feel the floor shake in its outcome.

I wrap my senses in their taste & gaze,
Unborn & imagined

I defy the daze
of unwrapped gaze
& imagine him releasing the confession.

THIS IS ME

I shake the nerves out & imagine the cure.
what makes the cure an essential part of the process
Does it spare you or save you?
Does it touch you or forget you?
Modify you to ask
"How do you determine your roots in the midst of fortune?"

The beats boomerang smooth sound
acquired by the steady rhythm of a response

"Be Safe…"

It's funny when we dare to care.

I've spent my whole life
shifted between pleasures of knowing & motions of connecting with others,
speaking for themselves while explaining the damage of others,
In an environment
I feel so fucking blessed with
& the tempting possessions to let it go
Pass it on
Creating a space for the new
while embracing a state of renouncing

I'd rather fall asleep

Stabilized >> Controlled >> Released.

CPSIA information can be obtained
at www.ICGtesting.com
Printed in the USA
BVHW081054171218
535792BV00002B/624/P